CW00656649

Brothers On Life™

Brothers On Life™

By

Matt Czuchry
Mike Czuchry

Zook Innovations LLC
Los Angeles California

Brothers On Life™

By
Matt Czuchry
Mike Czuchry

Editors
Angelique O'Neil
Nanci Grasso

Cover Illustration
Brian Rea

Consultants
Robert Wolff
Taylor Jones

Graphic Design
Betty Abrantes

Formatting
Lynette M. Smith

Published
May 01 2012

Print edition ISBN
978-0-9848452-0-0

Electronic edition ISBN
978-0-9848452-1-7

Library Of Congress Control Number
2011944312

Publisher
Zook Innovations LLC
9200 Sunset Blvd
Los Angeles CA 90069

To You

[C O N T E N T S]

ACT I 1

GEMS 2

DANDELIONS ON THE WIND 3

TAKING CHANCES 4

BLOOD BROTHERS 6

BULLDOZERS 10

CELEBRATE 14

FULFILLED 17

LOVE AND LIGHTS 18

FREEDOM 19

I WOULD 20

GOD LAUGHING 22

REIN 24

CREATION 26

DEITIES 28

UNRAVELING MYSTERIES 30

DESCARTES' DREAM 32

NIGHT LIGHT 33

COSMIC COMMUNICATIONS 34

LIKE A SUPERHERO 36

ARTISTIC EXPRESSION 38

JESUS' LAST BREATH 41

PAINT ON WINDOWS 42

A THOUSAND DREAMS 47

THE GREATEST 50

MIND OVER MAN 52

HURRICANES 53

SEEING ILLUSIONS 54

A LIGHT IN GANESHA 58

CLUES 61

[C O N T E N T S]

ACT II   63

TWO SIDES OF THE SAME COIN: SIDE ONE   64

TWO SIDES OF THE SAME COIN: SIDE TWO   65

THE YIN AND YANG OF DRINKING   66

WRONGS AND RIGHTS   68

PANDORA'S BOX   70

SPOTLIGHT   74

TOWERS   76

THOSE EYES   78

SAME EYES   80

TO BE   81

ONE   82

STICK UP FOR YOURSELF   84

A TROJAN HORSE   86

IN FLAMES   88

IN THE END   91

CRINKLES AROUND OUR EYES   92

TROUBLE   94

A GREAT SUCCESS: THE DARK SIDE   96

A GREAT SUCCESS: THE BRIGHT SIDE   98

THE JESTER   100

TRUTH ABSOLUTE   102

MERRY-GO-ROUND   104

ENOUGH   106

GENIES   108

THYSELF   110

BENT   114

CAPSIZED   115

LETTERS   116

IN THE MOURNING   118

BETTER BY YOU   119

PATHWAYS   120

[C O N T E N T S]

ACT III 123

EXPERIENCES 124

FLUSH 125

A BEAUTIFUL LIFE 126

BLISS 127

CONNECTED 128

BOTTLE IT UP 130

NEW DRESS 133

I LOVE 134

MAGNIFICENT 136

THE DREAMCATCHER 138

THE LIGHTHOUSE 141

THE DOC 144

SWEET TOOTH 146

PINWHEELS 149

THE CLOCK 150

END TO END 151

SHEDDING TEARS 152

EXTINGUISHED 153

HOMETOWN 154

HAPPY FACES 156

MY THINGS 157

BOUNDLESS 158

WHERE DO THESE SOULS GO 159

YOU'RE ALL I NEED 160

SPEECHLESS 161

HURRY UP 163

Johnson City, Tennessee, 1995. Counting the days till high school graduation. Watching the seconds on my alarm clock tick over. Hurrying life forward by waiting. Desiring a new life to come but not seeking it. In the face of rushing, my brother Mike quietly reminds me that we are promised no new day and each moment must be treasured because one will never know when death may come.

Into my right hand Mike slips me some of his original thoughts titled GEMS. These words on pieces of white notebook paper ring the alarm in my head. Buzzzz. I am up. Mike made me see as I was moving toward adulthood, I had forgotten an essential cornerstone of my childhood; the beauty of life embraced through imagination, dreams, and living in the moment.

My big brother Mike will always be my greatest friend. In our early youth after spitball fights and before our days became our dreams, we would end the night with a journey into our imagination. Surrounded by Beatles posters with Matt on the top bunk bed and Mike on the bottom one we would continue the family tradition by asking each other, "What story do you want to hear? The one about the motorcycle gang, the one about the gun, or the one about..." and then upon noting the story of choice, we would dive into a world without bounds. The fantastical characters we created within these stories would follow us into our dreams and continue to spark our creativity into our days.

Our summers in adolescence were spent on the beach even further away from the confines of reality. Dreams in the middle of the day were king as the chores on the sands were: 1) live fully 2) be in the moment 3) come up with a cool new superhero name, power, and cape. In these days where the salt air flowed through our veins, the only stress to endure was the unwelcome challenge of removing the beach sand from our bed sheets before sleeping.

As adults the lives we have individually created are quite different in appearance. Shaped through contrasting careers. Formed by distinctive cities and life experiences. Cultivated with a variety of loves. Our lives unique, yes. Opposing, no. Beginning with our first stories told from bunk beds through the book you have in your hand today, we both embrace the core perception that life is beautiful, challenging, precious, and an experience that interconnects us all.

In BROTHERS ON LIFE™ we share our stories with you as a vehicle to tap into the universal connectedness we all feel when experiencing the complexities of the mind and soul. Each piece is what you see. Each piece is what you need. All in an effort to unlock the dreams and imagination of that child within. Yearning for a life created, lived, and loved in the moment.

This book is dedicated to you.

Please begin.

New York City, 2012

Matt Czuchry

Mike Czuchry

ACT I

Mike and Matt, Londonderry, New Hampshire

Johnson City, Tennessee, 1995.

GEMS

Don't rush by the gems of today

To get to your tomorrows

That robbed yesterday

DANDELIONS ON THE WIND

For all the love we share this life and beyond
May it move through us and on to others
In each moment of goodness between us
Let it carry on the wind
Like dandelions

To new hearts
With each child born and life taken
We move into each other
Our souls connected
Forever alive

TAKING CHANCES

Even stars begin to fade as their traces are swept away

Even the sun will lose its sprite and darken

Time moves quickly and we age

But our souls never change

Who are we, whose heart can we touch

If we too are a mirage

We need to love

We need to give

But are afraid our love will not be taken

But hearts can dance

Given the chance

And a smile's spell

Can cast a shiver

If we are not afraid

To give

My big brother Mike will always be my greatest friend.

BLOOD BROTHERS

I can count on you
For anything and everything

Pushed down by foes and falling
Scratching my wrists, palms, and cheeks too
Salty tears clouding my eyes
These playgrounds of youth can be so unkind

I look to the sky for answers
Calling out for comfort to the clouds above
Alone

My eyes sweeping across the swings and ladders
Looking and searching to find
You

You run to me
Sweep me up in your arms
Show your teeth and fists to the world
And hug my pain away

You dry my tears
Remove my fears
And make it all okay

Even now, a touch older

My hands still bruise
My heart still aches
My soul still burns

And I still need you to pick me up when I fall

No matter the distance
No matter the space between us
I can still count on you
For anything and everything

I remember every scrape you healed for me
I remember every broken heart you sealed for me
I remember every battle you fought and won for me
I remember in sickness you stayed up through the night for me

When the time comes
And you find yourself in need of me
Call out to me

I will run to you
Fists ready, teeth sharpened, hugs loaded
I will sweep you up in my arms
Shed every last drop of blood for you

I will dry your tears
Remove your fears
And make it all okay

Trust in me
You will see
You can count on me
For anything and everything

Blood brothers

BULLDOZERS: PROLOGUE

I am walking in the middle of the road, splitting the white lines on the street while making my way to the set for work. It is pitch black at twelve o'clock at night. It is pouring rain and I am avoiding the puddles on my approach. I look up to see a giant bright yellow bulldozer creeping its way directly toward me. A couple of steps ahead I hear my friend say, "Oh my gosh, if my son saw this right now, he would be so happy!"

BULLDOZERS

Remember

Trucks, robots, dinosaurs, bulldozers
When we were kids
All we cared about
Were those fun horns, futuristic friends, silly feet, giant shovels

Those magical look up moments
Those bigger than us wow moments
No need as children to color inside the lines
No need to keep the sand within the boxes
Nothing could pause our spirit, except freeze tag

But things change when the world grows up

Fun horns become too loud
Futuristic friends turn into job takers
Silly feet become just plain silly
Bulldozers turn into traffic

Inevitably we grow
Does that mean the magic has to slip through our fingers
To be chased away and lost forever

Because actually
No matter the age
Dinosaurs are still pretty cool
And coloring between the lines at work will get you nowhere

Bulldoze my pretensions
Down to my essence
To the child within

To those magical moments
To those bigger than us wow moments

Remember

Matt

CELEBRATE

Will you come along
With me
Just for a moment

I can't die without
Without ever knowing
Without ever finding this love hiding within

I have to try
Try to love you
Try to love with eyes open
Diving in
Even if I fall in too deep
And we say farewell
I have to try

Better to have
Than to have not

I have to

Dance in the dark with you naked
Watch the candles flicker red in the pupils of your eyes

I need to

Drink too much by your side and
collapse on soft couches

I have to

Drink coffee under covers as you tell me of God
And spill Saturdays into Sundays

I need to

Bathe in your skin
With holy water sealing our wounds
Purifying our souls

Celebrate we must
For tomorrow is never promised

So we will make angels

Angels in the rain tonight
And when the rain turns to snow tomorrow
We will make angels in the flakes from Heaven
And when the snow turns to sun in the summertime
We will breathe angels onto glass windowpanes

No matter the weather
When feeling high
When feeling low
We can stay together
Forever

Our rainy days are better than sunny days
And our sunny days our souls complete

You are so much goodness, love, and beauty
Even if it all falls apart one day
If I tried
I can always say

Because of you
I danced in the dark
I laughed deeper
I loved like no other

For we are greatest in the moments that take our breath away
And any breath in between is just living

So come along with me
And let's celebrate

FULFILLED

Life
Will never be easy
For us

But

Life
Will always be full
With us

And

I need nothing more
Than us

LOVE AND LIGHTS

Girl what you do to me
In times like these
I am just lucky to be alive
With you here
In your embrace

Happiness
Flying throughout our souls
Calm and peace
Sprinkled throughout our hearts

Oh New York
What you do to me
These city streets
These city lights

Tomorrow
We will be
Shadows and dust
Indeed

But today
We are
Love and lights

FREEDOM

When you accept me

In my nakedness

At any moment

You make me

Free

I WOULD

I am as guilty as any other

In believing that my life should be worth something more
than theirs

But give me a choice

A real choice that will change the probabilities either for
or against my loved ones

And I would sell my soul to the devil to shift the odds even
if only slightly toward favoring your existence

Perhaps this is simply the expression of my selfish genes
and I am no hero in my actions here

But whether it be my twisted ambitions, genetics,
psychological reasons, or indeed true love

I would attempt to destroy all other living things, even my
own soul

If it meant one more second of your existence

Mike and Matt

GOD LAUGHING: PROLOGUE

When we are all gone who will have gotten it right,
the scientists or the theologians?

GOD LAUGHING

Here's my take on the universe

Stephen Hawking was right
There is no need for God to be in it

Richard Dawkins was right
God is an illusion

And yet there may very well be
Many universes
Outside of what we can measure

A funky world of multiple dimensions
Where you cannot rule out

God laughing
Just outside
Everything

REIN: PROLOGUE

New York City, August 27th, 2011. The radar on the television screen shows red swirls of Hurricane Irene approaching. For the first time in history Manhattan has issued mandatory evacuations of waterfront neighborhoods. I stay in the city, call two friends and say, "Come stay with me, let's not be alone." Water and food are stacked high in the white paint peeled cupboards. Bridges are closed and subways are shutdown. We are now stuck on the island. We had a choice, we made it. Now, it is up to the winds.

REIN

Raindrops can heal
Or
Wash away cities

We feel all powerful
But
When God decides to rein

We are reminded
We are tiny

CREATION

Ever want to split your soul
Into a million pieces

Perhaps that is what God did

For us
To live

Mike in birthday land

DEITIES

All these deities
Hanging out in my living room
Eating chocolate bars and drinking coffee
Spreading love, peace, and magic

Together we are never alone
Together we are free

The cross over my bed
Has no contentions
With Buddha in the garden

Ganesha on my mantle piece
Opens his arms
For Allah in the windowpane

Together we laugh
Together we sing

I kneel to all
Clean dust from all
Burn candles for all

In turn they lift me from my knees
Repair the wounds of my sins
And shower me with truth

UNRAVELING MYSTERIES

Properly applied and focused
The mind is capable of anything

Creating miracles
Unraveling mysteries
Outliving diagnoses
Making dreams come true

Yet most days
We are scared of the mind's possibilities
And remain bound to the expected

Often times
We create chaos subconsciously
Misdirecting our potential

We build a house of mirrors within us
Blurring reality
Making us think we are living fully
When in truth we are not

And like crabs in a bucket
We pull others down to ordinary with us

Delaying enlightenment
Facilitating ignorance
All in an effort to remain the same

DESCARTES' DREAM

The spirit of mathematics
Can explain
My soul
Exists

For Dad.

NIGHT LIGHT

Dad
Keep the night light on
For me
Please

Glowing

I need those halos of light
Cutting through the night
Protecting me from fear
Like a security blanket wrapped around my soul

Check under the bed
Make me believe
No monsters are underneath the bed frame
With their furry blue hair and sharp orange fangs
Ready to pounce on me

I need these white lights left on
Just as much as I need you

Nothing can protect me
From these monsters dancing in my head
Like your courage
And a light left on when you leave

COSMIC COMMUNICATIONS: PROLOGUE

After reading Brian Greene's "Fabric of the Cosmos" cover to cover twice, I am constantly moved by the notion of "spooky action at a distance." The principle states fundamental atoms of the universe once thought separate can be entangled regardless of the distance between them. Imagine if this theory was indeed proven true throughout all universes?

COSMIC COMMUNICATIONS

Consider this

Perhaps it is possible
To leave a trace
Of us

Beyond our own universe

Even if their galaxies do not share the same laws, like gravity

Perhaps

A cluster of signature atoms can indeed be arranged
Analogous to a crop circle

Connecting us to other universes
Like spooky action at a distance

To leave a trace
That in fact
We once existed

For my brother Mike.

LIKE A SUPERHERO

On your back
I will fly

Arms outspread
Pretending
To soar

And your shoulders
Are enough to carry my weight
For this life
And beyond

At the beach

ARTISTIC EXPRESSION: PROLOGUE

Dear Matt,

Listening to "Rise from the Shadows" by Alberta Cross and thinking of our spiritual road trip across the Icefields Parkway and on to Lake Peyto in the summer of 2010. A life changing moment.

Love you,

Mike.

ARTISTIC EXPRESSION

Sometimes painters capture a moment better than reality can

Expressing

A timeless consciousness that we all share

Capturing

The sadness you feel

The urge to pull the trigger found in a million itchy fingers

The rage
The hate
The grief
The fear
The happiness

We all feel this, all of this

Again and again

Like an old scratched-out vinyl record

This does not mean one's actions have been without purpose
just because we are all so similar

Perhaps all of our emotions mean more within the collective
than they ever could within one individual

I will say it again

Thank Buddha
Thank God
Thank all the painters
Thank The Beatles

Thanks to all who have captured and created our collective

JESUS' LAST BREATH

You and I

Just shared Jesus' last breath

And this is the beauty of our connectedness

PAINT ON WINDOWS: PROLOGUE

Europe, 2007.

I arrive at the airport bags in hand to find my niece in the back seat of the car. Her left eye is swollen shut, her eyelid blood red and popped out as large as a golf ball. This is far from normal. To the hospital we go. Two kids and three adults. The kids thinking nothing more than their Uncle Matt is here from the United States to play Chutes and Ladders. When my niece and her golf ball eye look my direction, she smiles brightly as if to say, "My eye is quite pretty, don't you think?" And I respond, "Looks like you got bitten by a giant mosquito over there. Darling, that bug probably popped after it sucked your eyelid dry." She laughs bold and bright. But, the adults know this is no mosquito bite. This is serious. This may be life and death. Toward the hospital we speed 50, 60, 70, 80mph....

PAINT ON WINDOWS

Caterpillar paint on hospital windows
Butterfly paint too

We pay to enter
The little one gives me a smile for free
And a dance to boot

Beds made up
One for me
One for mother and child
Make it all beautiful

Blankets firm and taught, the little one says
My eye is swollen shut, you see
And yet I can still laugh at you
Still I smile at you

Two more nights sleeping here
Then back home to play on slides tomorrow, she says
I am brave, she says
One hamburger, one cheeseburger to calm my nerves, she says

Simple things, big things
How do we divide the two
When thinking of dying
We must live every last second quick

Again on our way
Down these hospital halls
Hoping today is cleaner, fresher
So that our next day is louder, brighter

I will take you on my back
I will hold your hand
I promise I will protect your shadows that dance in the sun
All words spoken on the way
I believe them, she believes them

Our hands intertwine
Big and little
Big things, little things
I do not divide the two

We make our way down the halls
Stumbling on little chairs that line the walls
Believing the other is love so perfect

Even in the face of this struggle
We are safe
Our stinky feet and dirty toes enough to guide us
Guide us to the door

The door where others take my girl
Whisk her away, for you never have enough time
And now tubes take the place of my hands
As her care is no longer mine to give

Doors close
My mind drifts
I say to myself

No hospital can hold us
No needle can make us sad

For we are endless imagination
We are caterpillar paint on windows today
Yearning one day to be beautiful and fly free

Mike, June, 1975

A THOUSAND DREAMS: PROLOGUE

Vienna, 2007.

My agent calls to tell me "Gilmore Girls" has been cancelled. In the same breath she casually mentions I have not been cast in a movie I desperately wanted. I was in Europe trying my best to enjoy life and in the span of one call my career was turned on its head. Although I had my moments of doubt and battles with sorrow for sure, I believed that I was still on the right track with my aspirations. I knew my self deeply, I knew my soul, I knew my worth, and that calmed me. Even in this most challenging of moments, I knew I could work hard and survive this uncertain time. So why not dream a thousand dreams?

A THOUSAND DREAMS

Why not dream a thousand dreams
Of the true self I desire to become

Why not allow greatness to seep into my soul
To build fantasies upon fantasies
All in an effort to exceed the confines of my mind

Why not me
To be brilliant
To be free
To become my dreams in reality

In my imagination I have no chains
No end to my beliefs
I am boundless opportunity
King's castles in the clouds
Dragons for me to slay
As I become my favorite superhero

Flying free
Overcoming my vulnerability
No obstacle tall enough to derail me
No worry large enough to shake me

Magic in my bones
All conjured up through the electrical sparks of my brain

If I have to dream a thousand dreams to make this imagination become me

I will keep dreaming until sleep becomes me

Because
I believe
Life is indeed limitless possibility
Life is a dream made reality

Listening to Jay-Z's " Empire State of Mind " with a touch of whisky by my side.

THE GREATEST

In the beginning
Your new born fingers in my palms
I would whisper in your ear
You can be everything

The sun, the sky, the stars, the moon
Piercing every moment of darkness
With the greatness of your heart

Cradling you in my arms
I would always think to myself
I will be the inspiration that makes you more than you
Make you the greatest

Never realizing
From the beginning
I was the one placing shackles on your mind
Inhibiting your light that I desired all to see

Now I see
You must let go of me
Break free

It's okay
You can be without me
And still be everything for me

Just be
Shining bright enough out there for me to see
Becoming everything I ever wanted you to be

Believe in me
All you need is to be free of me
To become
The greatest

MIND OVER MAN

All these man made buildings
Crawling up through space
Infecting my peace of mind

Bricks and mortar
Wires and beams
Obscuring my view

Although I can't see the stars
I know they exist
Although I don't attain it today
I sense hope is upon me

Hope that all bad will become better
Hope that all better will become greater
Hope that all greater will become seen

Perspective knows
That created obstruction
Is soon to fall away
When the mind wins over the man made

HURRICANES

Brace yourself against the wind

And even when faced with hurricanes

Smoke that last cigarette

SEEING ILLUSIONS: PROLOGUE

One of the deepest relationships in my life was with a woman who has Stargardt's disease, a genetic eye disease that causes deterioration of the retina over time eventually leading to blindness. To compensate for her lack of sight, her brain fills in her vision of the world with information it thinks exists; even if in reality, the images are false. The result is a profound vision of life that is created through a mix of beautiful illusions, creativity, and the discovery of deep truths.

SEEING ILLUSIONS

Life like a prism
Our eyes, our brain
Creating reality
From a patchwork of electromagnetic energy

Your eyes
A bit different than most
Shaping reality from holes and incomplete light

Your brain
Compensating, adding, fabricating
Filling in the missing pieces from the blind spots

Your eyes, your brain
Together
Nurturing, fulfilling
A kaleidoscopic view of twisted reality

Mixes of illusions, truths, magic, and fantasy
Unreal or real
Who cares

You create life as it could be
You create life as it should be

Beyond merely capturing light from rods and cones
To creating and discovering the unseen
Rocking the fabrics of our beings to the core
Changing identities, essences, and beliefs

Like Alice in Wonderland
Yet no LSD on your tongue
Unlocking a door
Walking into a mystery
Powered only by imagination

Your eyes, your brain
Shaping a psychedelic symphony
Beyond the hearing of notes
To the seeing of colors
Blues, reds, and greens
And on to new hues undefined previously in all of history

In your eyes life itself emerges

Truths abstracted
Absolutes uncovered
Boundaries broken

And what do we call this new vision
All so much more than the simply seen
Unintentionalism

Real or unreal
Who cares
A word created by us
To define these stumbled upon truths
And serendipitous adventures
All actualized by your view

Your eyes like no other
Your brain like no other
Your vision like no other
Your world like no other

I wish everyone could see
Like you

Ganesha. A Hindu deity revered as the Remover of
Obstacles and Lord of Beginnings.

A LIGHT IN GANESHA

My eyes are open
Today

Strange things have come to me
Once in a dream
Twice as doubt
And a third time as reality

I now believe the greatest things once thought impossible
Are indeed possible
As you remove these obstacles from my mind

The world will move again
Tomorrow
Back to normal

Sun up
Sun down
Life will carry on
New obstacles will be reborn in my mind

But
I with purity
Move one foot in front of the other

I trust
That a path not there before
Will soon appear below my feet

As I walk
I place honey into my mouth
To sweeten my tongue
I know I must be kind in this moment
For people with doubt surround me
And claw at my beliefs

But
I remain calm
Knowing every man is a holy man
Blessing us on street corners with their tongues and fables
We only need to be wise to it
Eyes open
And treat them as if they too were Gods
I understand this new light within me

Rebirth
Renewal
Remover of Obstacles

I believe the greatest things once thought impossible
Are indeed possible

Sun up
Sun down
Obstacles come
And this too shall pass
No matter the doubt around me
My eyes remain open

Strange things have come to me
Once in a dream
Twice as doubt
And a third time as reality

CLUES

Nothing is ever as it seems

Things once thought **impossible** by geniuses yesterday

Are commonplace today

ACT II

Matt as Superman losing his powers

TWO SIDES OF THE SAME COIN: SIDE ONE

In the end

Nothing really happens

All of our actions

Swallowed up

Because of the universe

The pain

The anguish

Replaced

By darkness on all sides

Erasing

Us

TWO SIDES OF THE SAME COIN: SIDE TWO

In the end

Everything happens

All of our actions

Expand outward

Because of the universe

The joy

The brilliance

Magnified

By the sun from all sides

Nothing could ever erase

Us

THE YIN AND YANG OF DRINKING

They say drinking is bad

But Dean Martin felt sorry for those who never drank

Because he said, each morning they woke up and that was the best they could hope to feel all day

And it is true
Drinking has killed a few

It could kill me
It may kill you

Yet
It is not clear whether it is the drink that traps or frees you

Sometimes I suppose
The drink does both

But

How many years have you truly lived
The answer may surprise you

I would rather risk death to live
Than fear life and die anyway

WRONGS AND RIGHTS

Like when dreaming
And suddenly
Waking to the confusion of the morning light

I can't figure out
All of these wrongs and these rights

When living as a child sneaking around corners past your
bedtime
You might catch something beautiful
Like your dad praying on his knees
Rosary beads wrapped around his wrists

Or when living as an adult doing something foolish
You might find something breathtaking
Like true love

To me it seems
These wrongs always turn into rights
And my rights are perfectly forgettable

Like when dreaming
And suddenly
Waking to the confusion of the morning light

I can't figure out
All of these wrongs and these rights

PANDORA'S BOX

With naiveté as my most powerful weapon
I step forward
Making choices
Intending to save the world with passion

One tiny step
Sends pebbles rocketing throughout the universe
One justified calculation
Sends my theories into chaos

These doors now opened
Cannot be closed
These actions taken
Cannot be undone

In the presence of scepters and gold goblets
Good intentions first forged in the mind
Lose their way through neurons and dopamine
Eventually becoming ill-conceived contraptions

Malice aforethought is not a prerequisite
For opening Pandora's Box
Evil fingers are not a necessary characteristic
To pick the locks of stolen treasure

Everything I have ever done
Love was at the center
Yet sometimes love can be skewed

Great minds can destroy the world with brilliance
Pure hands can crumble nations with blankets
Religions can wage wars with faith

Sometimes deals with the devil are only seen in the
rearview mirror

I am asked to make decisions
Emboldened with guesstimates
And since I am only made of carbon and water
Life is certain to be ambivalent toward my misfortune

These lids now opened
Cannot be slammed shut
These measures taken
Cannot be undone

My first steps
My good intentions
Seemingly insignificant at the moment of inception
Carry the unintended weight of Pandora's Box

I tried to be scrupulous
I tried to be valiant
I tried

Yet through a series of unforeseen events
My life's bounty is given in the payment of forbidden fruits

And although my spirit never intended the evils
I will not deny myself the taste

Matt, Johnson City, Tennessee

SPOTLIGHT

With the filament pops
Come magic
Endorphins spike
Palms sweat
And the marrow within your bones begins to stir

In the spotlight

When the light begins to shine
It will at once humble you
And well you up enough to burst

In the spotlight

Some
Will be moved by your light
And run to your side
To give you shoulders to stand on
And hearts to lean on
Because they want to see you through to even brighter days

Others
Will have their reasons for darkness
They will run to your side
With their loose tongues
Rip through you and tear you down
Pushing you into the shadows
As they hoard your light for their own ends

Yet no matter what you do
Or who you are
Life will always give you both shields and arrows
Shoulders to perch on
And those loose tongues to cut you

You have heard it before
I'm here to echo the voices
And mirror the reflections

Don't be fooled by fools
All the jesters
May indeed be weeping behind their masks

Because
Life is never what it seems
In the spotlight

TOWERS

Even when we feel like steel
The right set of moments
Can make the towers come down
Leaving us bleeding
Raw
Real

Remember all those with pictures clasped in their hands
Hoping their loved ones would materialize out of thin air

Remember disbelieving
Watching
As fearful people
Jumped holding hands

And in an instant
They became heroes as they leapt

Seizing the moment to control their own fates
Refusing to be defined by others
Finding freedom from these towers

Is it worse to be those that have perished triumphantly
Or those clasping pictures left in waiting

Some may say
It does not matter
We all meet the same fate in the end

But perhaps our intuition was right all along
As Shakespeare said
The coward dies a thousand deaths
But perhaps what matters most
Is how we meet the one

August, 1992.

THOSE EYES

Once
I saw
A tear
Drop
The weight, the fullness
Expressing life itself
Seeing it fall
I, for all of time, make a commitment
To protect it
And I believe
Even when past my fingertips
Like an impossible pass
I can still catch it

To hold your tears
I will be miraculous
I will leap off buildings
I will dive in front of bullets
I will give you my life
All of it
Forever
I will cup my hands
Absorb your tears
Before the ground
Has a sense
That they've ever been shed

November, 2010.

SAME EYES

Pretty

Tears

Fall with the same weight

After all these years

Yet

Now sharpened

By time and your mind

They cut through my hands

Like knives

When they fall

From your eyes

TO BE

In your heart
There exist two worlds

Joy
And
Sorrow

They are always there
Together
Beating and working in concert

Blood spilled in one
Makes the other more vivid

We need both worlds
To be

ONE

How is it possible
That any one person
Could understand it all

Have all the answers
Lined within their pockets
To reach in and grab at a moment's notice
When the questions arise

Because
Answers are never facts
And
Questions are malleable

Because
Life is bigger than us
And
Life is all of us

Those lines drawn across countries
Are only real to those who aim to rule the world

The answer is lined within your pocket

Don't discard me because I am not you
We are all one within another
I am your soul now and always

STICK UP FOR YOURSELF

You can always cower in the corner
Again
And again
And again

If you choose that
If you want that

You can hide
From all the wrongs of the world
That beat you down
And then cover up the bruises on your face
As you carry on simply wishing life were different

But

Although pain is real
Suffering is choice

At some point
You must choose

To

Stick up for yourself
Even in the face of fists
Even in the face of doubts
Stick up for yourself

A TROJAN HORSE

Have we learned nothing
Hatred begins with merely words

Would it not be refreshing to just say

I love
I am
I hope to be
That is all

I remind myself to be gentle with words
Knowing without love and acceptance
It's easy to look for even the smallest of differences
As a way to slowly and subtly stroke our children's innocence
into prejudice

A TROJAN HORSE: POSTSCRIPT

Subtle prejudices seep into our very being even when we try to consciously prevent it. Test this theory by visiting a website titled Project Implicit at https://implicit.harvard.edu/implicit/. Click on demonstration and pick a topic or group you think you have no prejudice toward. You might be surprised at what you discover.

The authors have no association with this website, its contents, or the individuals who run this site.

IN FLAMES: PROLOGUE

Hermosa Beach, California, October, 2007.
Fires raging in the distance. Smoke in the clouds.
Rushing home to see if the flames have reached
my doorstep.

IN FLAMES

The sky is on fire
The city is on fire
The sun is bleeding
Dripping into the ocean

I shake off my sins
Place trust in my soul
Shake the trees of my entrapments
And watch the dew from the leaves drip into the ground
Is this dew enough to save me from the flames

I am thirsty
These tongues of flames have parched me
Thirsty for a clear Heaven
A white cloud
A blue sky
But the water is dry
For us all

The sky is on fire
The city is on fire
The sun is bleeding
Dripping into the ocean

Let the fires lap at my door but not enter
Let my will push them back
Let my courage spit on their sparks
Let my faith deny the fires of Hades

I wonder today
Who will perish in the ash and miss the city of gold
Who will be the lucky few to remain unscathed

Are these mere droplets of holy water from my tree
Enough to cleanse my doubt and mistakes
To save me
To be a lucky one

The sky is on fire
The city is on fire
The sun is bleeding
Dripping into the ocean

IN THE END

In the end

All that is and has been

Will be wrapped up in nothingness

Yet we defy the odds

With consciousness

And love

CRINKLES AROUND OUR EYES

Share your troubles
With me

No matter the weight
I will not buckle

With each tear shed
I welcome the pain

Knowing
In the end

We grow toward longer smiles
And perfect crinkles around our eyes

Mike

TROUBLE

When you were born
Your mother said you would be trouble

When I was a teenager
My father told me to be careful of women like you

Perhaps mothers and fathers may not know best
Because trouble or no trouble
I need you by my side to take on this crazy world

Your reckless psyche fends off the demons
Your erratic ways make me feel normal
And your devious smile keeps me alive

Even your faults make me hold your hand tighter
As your mistakes give me room to breath
And your burning force gives me the strength to challenge

Your mother was right
You are trouble
The best kind

I can't go at this world alone
This world of curveballs
I can't be everything on my own
This world of risk and loss

Who better to spin the world on its head
Than a woman born of trouble

A GREAT SUCCESS: THE DARK SIDE

In my mind as success arrives
The self becomes unnaturally exposed
Disconnected and contagious

All these good intentions
Twisted dangerously through pens and microphones
Become lost in the ether

Fear arrives as the outside world aims to distort my mouth
My heart once on my sleeve
Retracted from others to ensure vital statistics

From these dreams attained come delusions
Desiring to escape nightmares in my favorite secret haunts
Away from takers of souls toward givers of life

Arm and arm
Surround me with friendship
Let the wine drip from my lips and ease my toxins

Longing to hide
In the forts built as children
Away from the ink and empty audio of this adult world

As success arrives
I have become unnaturally exposed
Disconnected and contagious
Or have I

A GREAT SUCCESS: THE BRIGHT SIDE

In my mind as success arrives
The self becomes triumphantly lifted
Connected and heroic

All these good intentions
Personified perfectly through pens and microphones
Become found as universal truths now lost on no one

Happiness arrives as the outside world aims to kiss my mouth
My heart on my sleeve
Beating more deeply in shared vitality with others

From these dreams attained comes clarity
Fulfilled with freedom through my favorite public persona
Away from the self that takes toward the self that loves

Arm and arm
Surround me with riches
Let the joy drip from my lips and erase my toxins

Longing for nothing
In the way we lived as children
Embracing the colorful ink and beautiful audio of this adult
world

As success arrives
I have become triumphantly lifted
Connected and heroic
Or have I

THE JESTER

And when living life
Childlike innocence and laughter
Beats self scrutiny and doubt

And when dying
I would rather laugh amongst idiots
Than drown in seriousness

Mike

TRUTH ABSOLUTE: PROLOGUE

Dad once said, "If God could fit in my head, my God would be too small." Over time, I have come to believe we only comprehend a small portion of reality.

TRUTH ABSOLUTE

Being but part of a greater unknown

Each word from my lips

Equal in truth and equal in error

Each time that we speak

Truth becomes none the clearer

Through distorted illusions we peer at ourselves

And even though it all may seem real to me

Never mind this perception

Truth can't be known

But only

By truth alone

MERRY-GO-ROUND

So why can't I bite my tongue
Hold it deep in my throat
So as not to speak to you like an animal

True
It may be in reflex only
But still the barbs are no less spiny
Against my loved one
My loved one that I have loved for so long

These things I say from my mouth
And you say behind your teeth
Indeed all the jabs are colorful and perhaps necessary in a flurry
Yet later they remain deeper, distracted, and piercing

We are lucky
Time again gives us another chance to speak softly to each
other
And when the distance between us comes between the jabs
I sit alone behind my walls thinking

I ask for you
Call out to you
Deep in the night
Longing for you

Longing for you to come back to me
For you to be kind to me
Please

Walk softly down the hall on your return
With your arms held out wide
Freeing your chest and heart to me

See me before you naked and small
Both of us forgiving our instinct to hurt
All in an effort to be loved again
Fresh and new

For we are what we love
We are the ones closest to us
Defined by the other's eyes
Defined by the other's love

ENOUGH

No matter the love
No matter the hate

I just go on
Being me

And that
Is enough

Mike

GENIES

How many lamps filled with Genies can I rub
How many candles can I blow out
How many pennies can I skip across the ocean
Before my wishes come true

Wishing
Of you
Of me and you

These Genies from my palms could build armies
The dark smoke from my candles could burn down cities
These pennies drowning in the ocean could overflow vaults
And yet these Genies, candles, and pennies still don't equal you

If only, if only
These hours, months, and years of wishing left me with you

Without you
Tears are cathartic
As the soul needs a good soak

Without me and you
The sounds of love songs hold up my sanity
Listening, knowing, and feeling
That someone else traveled down my same path

Loved loftily
Lost mightily
And despite it all
Tried yet again

Summon the Genies
Light the candles
Unravel the penny rolls

Wishing again
Of you
Of me and you

THYSELF

I loved you so deeply
You were everything to me

My heart
My mind
My body
My soul

Wherever you were
That's where I wanted to be

Yet now
I love you no more
I feel nothing for you
You broke me

You were then
And this is now

You are but a mere reflection
In a distant sea
And I long not for you
Never again will I wish to explore your ebbs and tides

Who is new that I will love again
I know not
Who will make me shine
Who will make my toes curl with excitement

I hope for it
I fear finding it
I yearn for it
I don't know if I will ever be ready for it

When thinking of who I am in totality
Which time within me truly matters the most

The past, the now, the future

Life is all the moments that well up in our beings
No moment, no time
Is more important than the last
No kiss that has ever touched our lips
Is less than those still undiscovered

No stranger means less than those that love us
And even the ones who break our hearts
Still claim shattered pieces throughout our bodies forever

In life all of it matters
Everything matters
Everyone matters

The past, the now, the future

All woven together
To create
Thyself

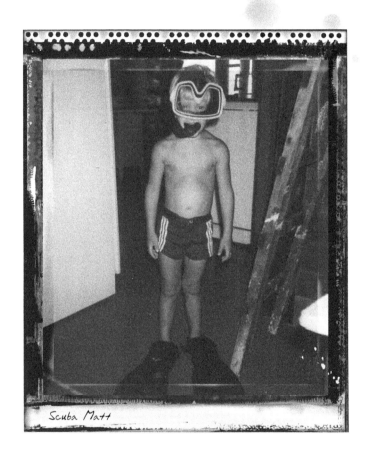

Scuba Matt

BENT

I lost myself
Within you
From the very first moment I met you

My life slipped into you
And I bent my existence
Far too much for you

I admit
It was all me and not you
I let you do all you tend to do
Because I desired you
I simply lost sight of what was what
And who was who

Now
I wonder if I could bend time
And twist the rules
Could I begin again with you
And yet not be owned by you

Because
I do want you
I still want you
But just the right amount of you

Music from Queen on in the background.

CAPSIZED

Adrift

In a sea of emotions

Waves pulsing through me

Sometimes wishing they succeed in breaking me

Is there more admiration for he who clutches on until saved

Or he who pushes off into uncertainty

Even if we desire our endings to be magnificent

Our demise may not capture these wishes

Whether it's this wave or the next

When feeling capsized

Water will always take our last breath

For that awkward thirteen year old within us all.

LETTERS

When you are near
I wish I could
Speak
But I can't

Your beauty
Is too much for me to bear

Please keep megaphones away from my lips
I don't want my vocal cords to be tempted

Tempted by you
To scream out
All the love I have to give you

Trust me

I feel my heart bursting for you
Through my chest
And on to the floor
Every single time
I see any little piece of you

I promise you

One day
You will find
A thousand letters
Strewn across my floor
All revealing
Everything that was felt for you but never spoken

IN THE MOURNING

I see you in my dreams

Even in my fantasies

I can't escape us

I continue to live a lie

I belong to you

Yet I live as if I belong elsewhere

And I know you too are lost

Nowhere

Like Eleanor Rigby

But I will be there

Mourning us

BETTER BY YOU

Maybe I could have made it work
Some fools do

Regardless

I know I could have done better by you

PATHWAYS: PROLOGUE

February 20th, 2011, 1:30 a.m.
Listening to John Lennon's " Mind Games."

PATHWAYS

Many of us wish
We had more than one life to live
Even a million

Because each storyline we changed
Or failed to follow
Could have been seen through

Even better to rewind and reset buttons
Correcting our imperfections
While contributing to the well-being of those we loved
Felt ambivalent toward
Or even hated

But perhaps
Life has meaning
Because we must live with all of our faults
And the bittersweet reality
That none of us
Got it just quite right

ACT III

Matt, Cape Cod, Massachusetts, 1984

EXPERIENCES

Only in having the courage
To taste
To feel
To try
Can you know
What it truly means to live

FLUSH

Flush
Through your veins
The rush of your most perfect day

Don't judge it, bask in it

Leave it

Untouched by that sour part of you

Let it

Slowly baptize
And convert
Each cell
Each atom
That comprise you

If only for a moment
Innocence remains

A BEAUTIFUL LIFE

A beautiful life
Is many lives
Led within one

So choose
From the gut

And
Move on

And
Live

Over and over
Again and again

BLISS

When things

Are most dim

Touch your skin

Trace slowly

Over your nerve endings

Then realize

No one else is feeling this

It is a unique experience

So tickle yourself to bliss

CONNECTED

Atoms twirl in tune with the universe

I sense I could tune into you

And expand myself a step closer to eternity

A cosmic blend of you and me

To relish a reality beyond comprehension

To know that we are really one

And the craziest idea is we are separated

By distance, by thoughts, by beliefs, by skin

All we need is to tap into the never ending surge of energies

Where atoms and planets and the entire universe

Weave together and connect like inseparable threads

Creating a grand tapestry

Blurring the lines of identity

No you nor I, just we

BOTTLE IT UP

Bottle it up
This moment to remember
Tangled up in bliss with you

We lie in peace, full, perfection

The madness around us simply echoes
Echoes that reverberate off the skyscrapers
And then stop still at the foot of our bed

This quiet you instill
Makes me see
The world is more beautiful when you are near

With every beat of life
You make me feel the joy of living

No doubts in me now
Love is everything
All that matters
And will prevail long after my time has come

For we are from

The same earth
The same sun
The same God
The same soul

Bottle it up
The beauty
Passion
Touches
Scents
My enlightenment

Scoop it all up
Our love

Fill all the glass bottles along the mantle
Fill every last one
Fill them to the tippy top

Our love will spill over
Unable to be held down by the rounded plastic caps
Let it

Let it
Trickle down the rippling glass sides
Down the fireplace
Into the cracks in the floorboard
To reach Hell below
Turning all those devils with horns and tridents
Into angels with halos and wings

I need not believe in God
To know
You are love's answer to evil

NEW DRESS

The way you wear that dress

I must confess

I am powerless

I thank the sun

For revealing

Everything

That little gap that brings in the light

Is such a wonderful delight

And breasts

Ridiculous

All I ask is

Wrap me up with a kiss

I LOVE

I love every freckle on your skin

I love how your red hair turns golden in the sun

I love how you snore in the night

I love how you wear those jeans with nothing underneath

I love how you embrace me with your body wrapped
around mine

I love how you smile or cry depending on any animal's
well-being

I love how you like the oddest looking things

Like me

I love how any imperfection becomes perfection in your eyes

I love how you make me appreciate me

I love that you have given me this chance to know you

I love how you have helped me conquer my fears

I love how you hug me even when my tears are random

I love you

Loving me

MAGNIFICENT

Sometimes it takes facing death
To finally listen to life
To know today
Is my only chance
To shine and be magnificent

Matt in the basement

THE DREAMCATCHER: PROLOGUE

I wrote this for a father and daughter. The daughter has gone through several major surgeries and on each occasion her attitude has always been through struggle comes strength.

THE DREAMCATCHER

Kisses on foreheads
Kisses on hearts
Kisses on wrists
Kisses on palms and on the back of hands too

Holding hands
We walk
Together
Bound
By everything that may come our way

Walking through the twists
Stumbling through the turns
Nicking our toes on pebbles
Scratching our knees on tree limbs

Bandage us up
With cartoon Band-Aids
And finish us off with warm lips to the skin
All raising the hairs on our tiny little arms with joy

And we move on
Through struggle
Comes strength
I once was told

And even though the blood seeps
Ever so slightly through the cartoon faces on our bandages
We move on
Hand and hand

So bandage me up
I am ready
I say it aloud again
I am ready
Bags packed

Armed with

Kisses on foreheads
Kisses on hearts
Kisses on wrists
Kisses on palms and on the back of hands too

Armed with

Your hand clasped in mine

THE LIGHTHOUSE

I don't have many moments left to spare for these thoughts
Lingering over words will only delay my emotion for you
So quickly I gather my quills, my wits, my limericks
All bound up together and etched across the accents of
burnt paper

I move swiftly with the ink
For these hours creep up on me
These fingers, these bones, these tendons grow tired from
my demands
As the hands of time do not move backwards

In time
Cities will crumble
These lights will flicker, one last burst before the dawn
And silence will prevail

But now
As in the beginning
And in the end

You are a lighthouse

When the fog blurs your pupils
And the rocks cut your toes
When the darkness covers your soul
And doubt prevails

When the ocean tumbles over the walls of your heart
And people around you betray you
When the ground sways beneath you
And welcomes intended are instead quite lonely

Remember
You are a lighthouse

You are
A light and a home
Glorious
And guidance
Hope
And comfort

For me
For yourself
And for others
You are a lighthouse

Even when the beams from our eyes dim
And our souls rise
When looking down from above

We will see
Still existing below

A lighthouse

Shining
Bursting
Lighting
Guiding
Teaching
Loving
Smiling
Igniting

And as waves crash around me

Quickly, I force the burnt papers inside my cloudy glass bottle
Send them across The Atlantic
For you, to you, about you
And reaching
You

Reaching
Reaching
Reaching

The lighthouse

New York City, June 2011.

This is written for a dear friend, a deeply spiritual man, who is facing open-heart surgery today.

THE DOC

If I never said it enough
I say it all now

With silence
Simply

My heart is open for you
To see

That beating life is precious
And one ought to be generous
With time
With people
With love

Coins are not currency
They are blessings
Beyond value held in this world

And honey
Shall not be taken for granted
Each drop shall be savored
For it is the sweetness of life that matters

I may weep
My eyes will soon dry
I may fall
I will rise

And it is life
That we must truly live
Not because of death
But because of life itself

With each beat of our hearts
We must live
With each movement of our souls
We must know there is something greater than us

Charleston, South Carolina, 2011.

SWEET TOOTH

And for birthdays
Candles
Cakes
And icing on my fingertips and lips
Sugar cones and orange soda
And all the innocence of youth spills throughout me

And for age
Over time my heart and bones ache
It's okay
My older hands slip around the curves of your body
And I remain a child always in your embrace
Still tangled up in the buzz of my youth

And for tongues
So many things left unsaid
If I could I would say it all
Enough said

And for love
Just give me five hours
A beach
A touch of salt water sprinkled on your skin
Some whiskey
And the sweet smell of flowers in your hair
And I will find a way to dance my way into your heart

February 28th, 1982

PINWHEELS

Where one begins

One ends

And yet another

Begins again

Only to eventually end

To allow for new beginnings

And this will always be

Until the end

THE CLOCK

Tick tock
The time you have left
Isn't much

No matter how hard we push against the clock
Eventually the cacophony of heartbeats
Will clash like a rusty tambourine

Seize
Block
Bleed

God and nature working together
Both busy
Little by little
Erasing us to dust
So armor up
Ready your souls
For the battle of life

Tick tock
The time you have left
Isn't much

END TO END

I have high hopes of getting older
Most say life gets harder with age
But it also gets grander, more real

Real at both ends

On one
Fear

The other
Peace

End to end
Every bit of it, all of it
Real

Will the fear tear us apart
Or will it birth humble perspective

I have high hopes
Of getting older
That as we move closer to the end
Life will become clearer
As we rediscover the peace of that child within

SHEDDING TEARS

I am shedding tears tonight
For dictators and heroes alike

A human being's last moments
Should not be met with

Atrocity
Nor
Mockery

Guardians of good and protectors of evil
Though different in aspirations
Are still souls of this world

Upon exiting life
The deepest love is shown
In seeking compassion when our hearts are full of contempt

EXTINGUISHED

With light
There are shadows
And it is the darkness I fear
A life without being
Is being nowhere
The flame from a candle
Will too soon wisp away
To faint traces of smoke
And even less in the end
And though it did burn
And give light
All must surrender
In time
To the night

HOMETOWN

In my hometown

I take the skeleton key in my hands
Travel down the stairs with my toes
View the dusty shoeboxes filled with Polaroids with my eyes
And unlock the trunk with my courage

Dust off the film reels
Come back with popcorn in my mouth
Soda pop for my pops
Some Junior Mints for Junior
Sweets for Dad's sweetheart
And cotton candy for K

As I unlock my soul with a wink
Perforated film strips begin to turn
Turning over the rusty wheels of the projector
Creating dancing images on the stained white walls

Movies of all of us
Childhood stories being told in silence
Our hearts beating loud in unison

I see youth flash before my eyes
Watching life unravel hand and hand with grandparents
All this too soon to be gone
Yet we never know how to say goodbye

There are too many beginnings in a day
To fully comprehend our endings when they come
But the honesty of life always refuses to be denied

These footsteps my mother leaves in her wake
Will be walked in by her sons and daughters

That is the way it works
At least in my hometown

So now
I ask of you
Nothing more than I ask of myself

In your hometown

Take the skeleton key in your hands
Travel down the stairs with your toes
View the dusty shoeboxes filled with Polaroids with your eyes
And unlock the trunk with your courage

HAPPY FACES

Your lasting success
Is not counted
By the silver
You hold
In your clutches
To safely tarnish

But rather

Your worth
Is measured
By the hands
You grasp
Through suffering
To effect luminescence

MY THINGS

All these material things
I have collected
Are indeed immaterial
You can pile them up
And float them to the sky

When I am gone
My mark will be left
In hearts
In sand
In the eyes of my children

When my body slips into the earth
Others will stay
To collect my things
My many things
You can pile them up
And float them to the sky

All these things
These many things
We can do without

BOUNDLESS

I am not my mind

I am not my body

I am my soul

And our souls are everything

For Mom.

WHERE DO THESE SOULS GO

Where do these souls go that leave us
Do they come around and back again
Or do they leave us for good

So when I go to bed tonight
Tuck me in with some dust from the Sandman
And leave me with kisses and hugs to hold forever

Because we know not
When or where our hearts will end
So love me

Because we know not
When or where our souls go
So comfort me

Leave me with kisses and hugs to hold forever
Until we are all given back
To where it is we were before

YOU'RE ALL I NEED

Count me in
Leave no doubt in your eyes
I will stop the tides to save you
I will shake the moon from the sky to please you

Even at an arm's length
You're all I need
Even an earshot away
You're enough

When my body decays
The soil living off my years
I will leave my spirit in pictures to heal you
I will shake the rubble with my soul to love you

Love you from an arm's length
Love you from an earshot away
Even when I am gone

Listening to " Love Lost."

SPEECHLESS

I have something to say
Even if the words don't come today
Swirling confusion
Damn this brain, it misfires
Leaving me speechless
Decaying neurology
Fragile like cloth
Eaten by moths
Lost
Wandering
But I do remember this
I love you

Matt as Superman regaining his powers

Hurry up
and live...

MATT CZUCHRY

Having spent twelve years as an actor in film, television, and on stage, Matt Czuchry brings his unique perspective on the human experience to BROTHERS ON LIFE™.

EDUCATION:

College of Charleston, 1999. Graduated Summa Cum Laude. Matt Czuchry received the Bishop Robert Smith Award upon graduation from College of Charleston. This award is the highest honor given to a graduating senior and represents valued contributions in academics, sports, and throughout the Charleston South Carolina community.

CAREER HIGHLIGHTS:

Czuchry is currently filming his third season on the two time Emmy® nominated drama, THE GOOD WIFE. Czuchry received the 2011 Entertainment Weekly Best Supporting Actor EWwy and has earned SAG ensemble nominations in 2010, 2011, and 2012 for his work on the hit series.

In 2009, Czuchry played the lead character of Tucker Max in I HOPE THEY SERVE BEER IN HELL. The book by the same name was a New York Times bestseller for three years and remains a cult classic.

In 2008, Czuchry starred in the second season of the critically acclaimed television series FRIDAY NIGHT LIGHTS.

In 2007, Czuchry was on stage in the title role of Wendy Wasserstein's West Coast premier run of the play THIRD.

Beginning in 2004, Czuchry spent three seasons as the character Logan Huntzberger on the hit series GILMORE GIRLS. Czuchry received three Teen Choice nominations for his role on the beloved series.

MIKE CZUCHRY

Mike Czuchry is currently an Assistant Professor of Psychology at a small liberal arts college in Texas. He has over fifteen years of teaching and research experience. He has received both teaching and research awards from students and colleagues.

EDUCATION:

Mike received his B.A. in Psychology from Colorado College in 1990, his M.A. in Experimental Psychology from East Tennessee State University in 1992, and his Ph.D. in Experimental Psychology from Texas Christian University in 1996.

TEACHING:

Mike teaches Introduction to Psychology, Cognition (how we think, learn, remember, and solve problems creatively), Quantitative Methods (applying statistical techniques and research design to understanding phenomena), History & Systems of Psychology, as well as Sleeping & Dreaming.

RESEARCH:

Mike has a variety of research interests but is particularly intrigued by developing and evaluating games and other motivational and thinking techniques that can be used to improve learning, treatment, and quality of life.

PUBLICATIONS AND PRESENTATIONS:

Mike has over twenty peer-reviewed publications, and over ninety combined presentations at regional, national, and international conferences.

Lightning Source UK Ltd.
Milton Keynes UK
UKHW040640070519
342237UK00001BA/340/P